IMAGES
of Scotland

LINWOOD

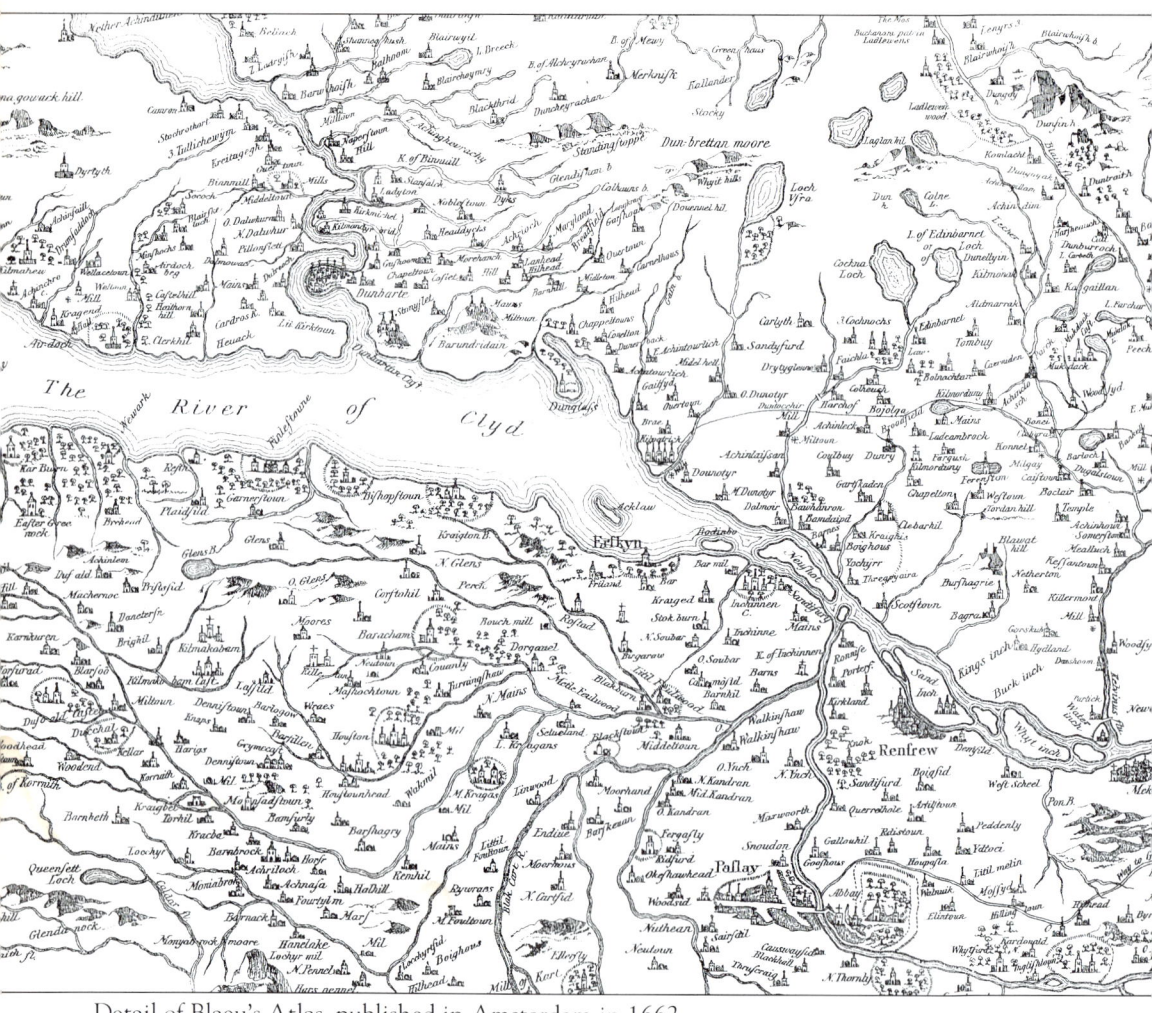

Detail of Blaeu's Atlas, published in Amsterdam in 1662.

IMAGES of Scotland
LINWOOD

Compiled by
James Winters

TEMPUS

First published 1999
Copyright © James Winters, 1999

Tempus Publishing Limited
The Mill, Brimscombe Port,
Stroud, Gloucestershire, GL5 2QG

ISBN 0 7524 1581 6

Typesetting and origination by
Tempus Publishing Limited
Printed in Great Britain by
Midway Clark Printing, Wiltshire

Contents

Acknowledgements		6
Introduction		7
1.	Agricultural Scenes	9
2.	Trade and Industry	19
3.	Local Mansions	39
4.	Churches	49
5.	Streets and Buildings	63
6.	Social and Leisure	89
7.	Institutions	103
8.	The Car Plant	113
9.	Inkerman	125

Bibliography

Crawford & Semple; *The History of the Shire of Renfrew*.
McKenzie, Reverend Robert D., BD; *Kilbarchan - A Parish History*.
Millar, A.D.; *Castles and Mansions of Renfrewshire*.
Stewart, Alexander M.; *Chronicles of the Stickleback Club*.
Hector, William; *The Judicial Records of Renfrewshire*.

Acknowledgements

The author would like to thank the following people for their help and permission in using their photographs.
Mr Robert Law, Mrs Mary Inglis, Mrs Rose McAree, Mrs Isa Craig, Mr George Dickson, Mr John Reid, Mr Robert Leitch, Mrs Janet Craig, Mrs Margaret Rennie, Mr J. Rowand, Mr Roger Blackwood, Mr Robert Corrigan, Mrs Maria O'Neil, Paisley Museum and Linwood Library.

Introduction

Situated about two miles east of Paisley, the village of Linwood (its name means the 'pool in the wood') is nearly always prefixed as The Linwood. The reason for the prefix probably dates back to the fourteenth century when Linwood consisted of a small collection of farms and dwellings concentrated on the banks of the River Black Cart. It was given the collective name – The Linwood, with early maps showing it as Ye Lynwode. The land on which Linwood stood was owned by Paisley Abbey, which was founded in the twelfth century. One of its many assets was the fishing rights on the R3iver Black Cart. Granted by the charter of William the Lion, they in turn rented them to the people of Linwood who had a cruive (salmon trap) at the weir at Linclive.

The villagers paid for these fishings along with their tithes at the grange at Blackston House, wherein resided Abbot George Shaw (1472-1498). Linwood at the time was an agricultural community and remained so for centuries, but all was soon to change with the coming of the Industrial Revolution. In 1792 work began on the cotton mill in Napier Street, described at the time as 'the most splendid establishment in the cotton spinning business, perhaps in Britain.' By 1794 a regular town on an elegant plan was already in the course of erection. The minister of Kilbarchan Parish on talking of the new mill said 'a work of this sort is a school where the children of the poor, otherwise a burden upon their parents, may be trained to industry and virtue.' A smaller cotton mill known as Henderson's, along with a print mill owned by Paterson and Neilston, who printed Paisley shawls, was also built in Napier Street. This brought a lot of employment to the village and expansion soon followed. The village consisted of two streets, Napier Street and Bridge Street, until further houses were built in the 1920s and 1930s.

Another industry that began developing was mining. Pits soon began to spring up in and around the village. The employment provided by these industries was soon taken up by immigrants, mostly from the Highlands and Ireland, the latter arriving to escape the terrible famine caused by the failure of their crops due to potato blight. In 1855 several rows of houses were built just off Bridge Street and named The Redan after the battle in the Crimean War. About a half a mile north-west was another mining community named Balaclava, built in the area known as Clippens, while yet another mining village, this time a mile to the east was born. This too was named after a battle in the Crimea, Inkerman, and like the other two it consisted of four rows of houses, a school and a company store.

With the coming of the American Civil War the cotton trade was denied its supplies of raw material and this brought about a slump in trade followed by the closure of some mills. Linwood mill survived until 1872, when it finally closed down. Later that year it reopened as a paper mill under the ownership of R. & W. Watson, who manufactured all manner of papers, including one called LINSON, which joins the first three letters of LINwood and the last three letters of WatSON.

Engineering played an important role in the development of the village. In 1897, W.J. Hart Reid founded the Reid Gear Company in the old Picking Hall of Henderson's mill, which had suffered a fire. Their new premises were at the foot of Napier Street. They made a wide range of gears for all industries, including the Royal Navy.

In 1914, Dent and Johnston & Company took over the old Eclipse Tool Company's works when they were merged with the Reid Gear Company. Dent's, as it was known, made high quality scientific instruments, with the London branch of Dent's making the clock mechanism in the tower of Big Ben.

In the latter part of the nineteenth century, the Clippens Shale Oil Mining and Distillation Company was formed, distilling mineral oil from shale deposits by a process invented by James 'Paraffin' Young, who stayed for a short time at Clippens House.

The founding of the Galbraith groceries and provision empire began from a small shop in Napier Street and went on to become a vast empire before being swallowed up by a large supermarket chain.

In 1960 the Rootes Motor Company were invited to come to Linwood to make Scotland's car – the Hillman Imp. The thousands of jobs this created brought in workers from all over and in order to house them and at the same time alleviate Glasgow's housing overspill, many of them settled in Linwood. In a short space of time the population exploded from 2,500 to 1,5000 and what had been a small village expanded to become the thriving town it is today.

The most difficult part of writing this potted history of Linwood has been not what to include, but what to leave out. I have enjoyed every minute of research and collating the information. I hope that Linwoodians at home and abroad enjoy looking through its pages and reminiscing at, The Linwood.

One
Agricultural Scenes

Candrens Farm, c. 1903. This farm, built on low-lying ground near Inkerman on the road to Linwood, was prone to flooding and had to be rebuilt on a better location nearby. The farm has for many generations been in the hands of the Rowand family.

Candrens Farm. Rebuilt using some of the stonework from the previous farm on a more favourable piece of land.

Greenfarm, c.1950. This farm dates back many centuries and is mentioned in the poll tax rolls of 1695. When this photograph was taken it belonged to Mr George Craig, (you can see a large G.C., his initials, in the slates on the roof above the dormer window on the left). The farm was demolished in the early 1960s and the new church of Saint Conval was built on the site.

Middleton Farm, 1974. There has been a farm on this site since the sixteenth century. Little Middleton stood near the River Black Cart but has long since gone. In 1768 there was a great thread bleachfield at Middleton belonging to James Semple Jnr. The farmer for many years was William Kerr, succeeded by his son James, who has since retired and sold the farm to a business concern that grows turf for commercial purposes.

Auchans Farm, 1974. The lands of Auchans date back to 1225, but changed hands by charter in 1591 to the Abercorn Family, along with Middleton, Lynwode, Rywrayis, Wyndiehillis and Mureheid. The farm for many years was in the possession of Mr John Young, who eventually retired and sold the property.

East Fulton Farm, 1974. The land and farm at East Fulton go back many years into history. The present farm is owned by Mr Alan Stirling, who runs a haulage business from there.

Clippens Farm and Villa, c. 1950. Clippens Farm was the home farm for Clippens Estate. Last farmed by the Stirling family in the 1960s, it was acquired by Renfrewshire Council and converted into a depot for their parks department. Clippens Villa was occupied by a Mr Tervit in the 1880s, a manager at the nearby oilworks. The building later became the farmhouse and is now owned by Renfrewshire Council.

Knowes Farm, situated on the south bank of the River Gryffe. In 1860 this land was farmed by Tom Sibbald. Adjacent to the farm was a wooden footbridge over the river which took the form of a single span Gothic arch, known locally as the 'Tattie Howkers Brig' because of its use by seasonal farm labourers moving from farm to farm. The bridge was carried away by the great winter flood of 1879 and never rebuilt. The Knowes has since been converted into a private residence.

Nethercraigends Farm. At one time it belonged to the powerful Cunningham family of Craigends House. Situated by the Ard Gryffe where there is a ford across the river, there was until quite recently a series of stepping stones next to the ford, which have since disappeared.

Selvieland Farm. Mentioned in the poll tax rolls of 1965 but probably much older. It was sited on the south bank of the Gryffe, about a mile downstream from the Knowes. Access from the Georgetown Road was across the river via a steel bridge designed by Sir William Arrol.

Linwood Moss, c. 1860. This ploughman proudly stands by his pair of horses. The ploughman of his day considered himself to be the elite among the farm workers – his skills certainly confirm this belief.

Mr John Reid in North Drive, c. 1930. Mr Reid had a milk delivery business with stabling in Rosebank Yard at the top of Duke Street. He also stayed in Ryewraes near Clippens and latterly farmed at Threeply in Bridge of Weir. His son, John, has a road haulage business in Napier Street.

Sandy McKenzie poses for the camera in North Drive, c. 1930. The houses behind the cart are in Bridge of Weir Road.

Mr John Reid prepares one of his horses for a show, c. 1930.

Clydesdales were the favoured horse for all manner of tasks and on a show day they had a well-earned rest as their owners primped and fussed over their appearance.

John Reid's brother, Robert, lends a hand as another Clydesdale is ready for the show.

Ryewraes, c.1930. Another of John Reid's horses is shown to the camera. Behind the wall in the background is the walled garden at Clippens House. The name Ryewraes, like Clippens, dates back a millennium but did not become recorded until 1547 when it was occupied by John Caldwell. In the 1880s its cottages were used to house transient workers who worked in the shale oil industry at Clippens. By the turn of the century the oil industry and its associated pits had gone.

Linwood Goods Station, c. 1930. Charlie McCurday with his horse and cart loaded with coal dross destined for the boilers in Watson's paper mill. Shortly afterwards, the job was being done by a Sentinel steam wagon.

Napier Street, c.1890. Andrew McAree with his sour milk cart. He was employed by Robert Kerr of East Fulton, who sold milk in pints and quarts. The small girl is thought to be one of the Galbraith family.

Two
Trade and Industry

The Reid Gear Company, c. 1920. A selection of cut gears appear in the the foreground of the picture.

The Engine Room for number 1 Pit, East Fulton. This building was all that remained of the mining industry and was demolished in 1995. It originally housed the engine to raise and lower the cages up and down the pit. The building was used latterly by Todd & Dickson, who began a joinery and carpentry business in an old cowshed next to the public park.

The pits around the Clippens area were mostly mining ironstone. Shale was a by-product that was heaped in bings like this one at Number 1 Pit at East Fulton. The primary goal was blackband and blueband ironstone. The shale was considered worthless until James 'Paraffin' Young discovered that mineral oil could be extracted by a process of distillation, and by the mid-1880s the Clippens Shale Oil Company was in full swing. Before 1900 it had vanished but the local brickworks used the spent shale (after the oil had been extracted from it) to make blaes bricks.

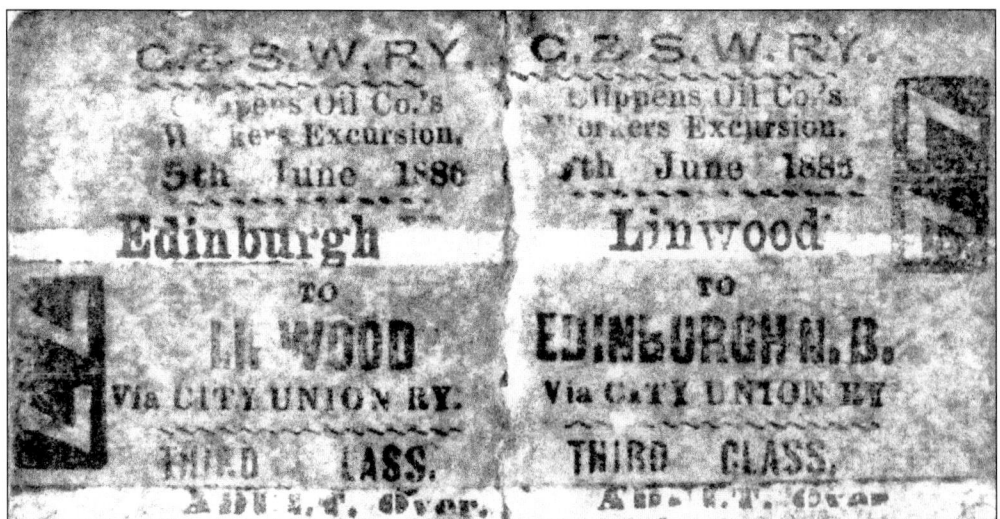

It was a hard life in the oilworks but the workers were treated now and again as can be seen from this railway ticket. It reads:
GLASGOW & SOUTH WESTERN RAILWAY.
CLIPPENS OIL Co's WORKERS EXCURSION
5th JUNE 1886
LINWOOD TO EDINBURGH VIA CITY UNION R.Y.
THIRD CLASS ADULT.

Behind this building in Bridge Street was situated Dunlop's Pit, owned by Mr Dunlop, who was an ironmaster and manufacturer of waterwheels (one of his wheels is still in existence at Eaglesham). Dunlop Street, which adjoins the pit, was named after him. The building was once owned by a Mr Elliot who had a carting business there. Mr Elliot also ran an ambulance service from here and anyone unlucky enough to fall ill was placed in the back of a horse-drawn wagonette, covered with a blanket and then taken to the hospital. The firm of Donaldson started a business specializing in agricultural and grasscutting machines. In the 1960s it was also a garage and filling station. More recently it became Scotia Trading Services.

The old Caledonian Railway branch line came into the village from the east, past Blackston and Middleton and ending in the goods yard beside the above building. There was a small tramline that crossed from the goods station across Bridge Street, up past the Masonic Hall and off to Barrowman's Pit. The line suffered under Dr Beechings axe in the 1960s and was closed down.

The branch line from the west into the village terminated behind the old parish church, just visible on the left above the trees. This line was the Glasgow & South Western Railway. The chimneys on the right are the paper mills.

The Old Cotton Mill, Linwood

Linwood Cotton Spinning Mill. Built in 1792 and destroyed by fire in 1802, the mill was rebuilt in 1805 using cast iron for its construction to render it 'incombustable'. The building was six storeys with garrets (attics) and boasted 540 glass windows and had 28,000 working spindles. It was to employ 1,800 workers but in reality fell short of this target. The minister of Kilbarchan Parish (to which Linwood belonged to at that time) said: 'A work of this kind is like a school in which the children of the poor, otherwise a burden upon their parents, may be trained to industry and virtue.' The power to work the mill came from two water wheels – one was an overshot wheel and it can be seen in the foreground in a cloud of spray. The other wheel was on the other side of the building and was operated by the tide coming up the River Black Cart. This along with a steam donkey engine supplemented the horsepower available. The poor output of the wheels was of concern to the owners who then called on the services of William Fairbairn. Fairbairn was born in Kelso and became a civil engineer of note and an expert in stresses in cast iron. He redesigned the buckets and patented this 'ventilated bucket' design which allowed the water rushing in to gain egress through holes in the bucket and thus improve the power and efficiency of the wheel. Fairbairn was later knighted. In the mid-nineteenth century the cotton mill along with most others went into decline due to the lack of raw cotton brought about by the American Civil War, and was finally closed in early 1872. In July of the same year it was taken over by R. & W. Watson Brothers, who opened up as papermakers.

Paper was made by cutting up rags and old cloth. This was done high up in the Rag Loft and here we see the foreman with his squad of women workers around 1895, dressed in their 'thibbet aprons'. Thibbet was a corrupt form of Tibet, where the rough wool material was produced. The foreman at the back is Tom McMeekin. The lady on the front left is Anne Reid, then Jessie Edminson, and fifth from the left is Agnes Hannah McMeekin.

Adding colour and dye by hand into a batch of minced pulp and rags in these huge vats is a process that was later done by machine.

Automated colouring and dyeing.

September 1959. Paper was embossed with many finishes – here is a three roll embosser.

25

Tommy Inglis at is Number 3 rolling mill.

The end product as it comes off the rolling mill.

A worker takes off his shoes and enjoys a break.

R. & W. Watson's Sentinel steam wagon in the goods yard in 1930. The wagon is loaded with coal dross to fire the boilers in the mill. The men are from left to right: shovelmen W. McKay, W. Stevenson, J. Corrigan and the driver, J. McGuinness.

By the 1950s, Watson's steam wagon had been replaced by the Albion lorry seen here at the goods station. The man in the centre is Bobby Gilmour.

Inside the power room in the paper mill. The days of water and steam power have gone with electricity now providing the power for a modern industry. Electricity was first used commercially by Reid Gear Co. in 1914 when they became the first company to use electric power supplied by the newly formed Clyde Valley Electric Power Company. The man in the picture is Mr Templeton.

Since the beginning of industrial employment and long before we had social security and a health service, employers did not worry too much over the welfare of their employees. If you were unfortunate to be sick or absent from your job there was no sick pay or wages to rely on. The workers in the paper mill formed their own sickness benefit society whereby each worker paid a small sum of money into the society each week. If they were unable to work through sickness or injury they received 3/- (15p) per week, but if your illness confined you to bed the benefit was 6/- (30p) per week. People were watched in secret by society members to limit abuse of the system and ensure that they were not claiming the higher rate when not actually confined to bed – perhaps the modern social security learned this method of snooping from Linwood?

Every year, during the annual Paisley Fair holidays, the mill lade was drained for maintenance purposes. Here in 1930, a squad of workmen are building a new sluice to improve the flow to the mill. The men are from left to right, back row: -?-, Benny McGroarty, -?-, William Roach, -?-, -?-, Robert Ross (Joiner/Millwright), -?-, -?-, John Dickson (Joiner/Millwright), -?-, Front: Will Connell (Joiner/Millwright), -?-, -?-, -?-, -?-, -?-, W. Stockman (below).

In 1972, as part of its centenary celebrations, R. & W. Watson exported a load of Linson paper to Tokyo. Linson paper was invented in 1936 in the mill laboratory, using a mangle belonging to the chemist's wife. It was intended to replace bookcloth as a binding material. The paper was at first unpopular because nobody believed that paper could be as strong and hard-wearing as bookcloth. Eventually London County Council pioneered the way by binding all its books with Linson. All the big companies like W.H. Smith followed suit when the paper proved to be as good, if not better than bookcloth, and it was exported to over fifty countries. Watson's also invented the use of paper to insulate copper cables and made a vast range of papers for industry, including paper for Jacquard Looms in the textile business.

The shipment of Linson reaches the docks and is loaded, bound for Tokyo. Two years later Watson's became part of the Tullis Russell Group, based in Fife, and papermaking virtually ceased at Linwood. They now emboss and finish papers to a high quality – one of the many products using this type of paper is the board game Trivial Pursuit.

Built around 1909, this building in Bridge of Weir Road began life as the Eclipse Tool Company (manufacturing machine tools, mainly lathes, but they also had a small lead-rolling mill). In 1910 the Eclipse Co. planned to set up in car production as the Linwood Motor Manufacturing Company, but owing to lack of capital investment it fell through. In 1912 the company was taken over and absorbed by the Reid Gear Company. The following year the building was opened as Messrs Dent & Johnson Ltd, makers of precision scientific instruments and manufacturers of navigational equipment for the RAF and the Navy during the war years. The London branch of Dent & Company made the tower clock in Big Ben. The process in making the dials of the instruments luminous involved using radium, which is radioactive. This had built up in the ground under the factory. In 1974 the factory was demolished and the rubble and soil were taken away for disposal. The site remains today as a green field and is still monitored for radioactivity.

Looking up Duke Street we see Dent & Johnson's canteen – the building behind is now the Gordon Anderson Plant, but before, it was a small foundry. During the Second World War it was used as a cinema. In the foreground is a Hillman Imp. On the right hand side of Duke Street, before the Golden Pheasant Hotel was built, was a small grassy hill known locally as 'Daisy Hill'. It was the site of a mass grave when in the 1850s a terrible outbreak of cholera swept through the area killing hundreds of people. The Linwood victims were buried at 'Daisy Hill'. The hotel, which was built on the site in the 1960s, is reputed to be haunted.

One of the many types of lathe made by the Eclipse Tool Company – this one is a surface and boring lathe.

Another lathe inside the Eclipse works, c. 1912.

The Eclipse Lead Rolling Mill, 1910. The lead was made into all manner of pipes and bends for the plumbing industry, but it disappeared when it was taken over by the Reid Gear Company in 1912.

Founded in 1897 by William J. Hart Reid and utilizing the picking hall of Henderson's Cotton Mill, the company specialized in precision gear-cutting and manufacture. They moved to their present site at the top of Napier Street in 1907. The company makes gears for a wide range of applications from a few inches to eighteen feet in diameter. The Royal Navy use their gears in deck machinery. In the 1960s the firm was taken over by Thomas Reid of Paisley, who also made gears. They were, however, no relation to the original founder in whose honour Hart Street was named.

A selection of cut gears with others in the process of cutting – note the two women (middle left) who were probably working there as part of the war effort, as the photograph was taken during the the First World War.

Looking along a line of lathes and cutters, most of which were made by the Eclipse Tool Company.

All the power for the machines was provided by an overhead belt drive, most of which were unguarded. The men are wearing flat caps known as 'doolanders', as to a man they all look to the camera.

Mickey Brogan, standing on the left, beside the new works lorry, c. 1950.

Linwood Co-operative Society was formed in October 1871 and began with a small shop and bakehouse in Napier Street. In 1925 they opened the premises shown above in Bridge Street. The lady second from the left is Minnie Grossart and fourth from the left is Dave Smith, while next to him is Annie McPhee.

United Co-operative Services bakers van in Napier Street in 1914. James Dickson is second from the right.

Galbraith's Stores Ltd, began in a small shop in Napier Street and was started by John Galbraith whose aim was to provide quality groceries and provisions at a reasonable price to the villagers. From this small beginning Galbraiths grew to become a vast empire. The firm grew with the take-over of Cochrane's to become Galbraith-Cochrane. They have both since been taken over by a vast dairy concern. The shop in Napier Street lies semi-derelict at present.

Harry Price stands beside his Unic delivery van in 1926.

The sawmill, founded by James Kennedy in 1951, was on the right, behind the fence. In 1855 the area was a small mining community called Balaclava. It consisted of some rows of cottages, a school and a small shop owned by Mr Weeple. The school closed in 1874 and the pupils were transferred to Linwood. In addition to selling the miners' groceries, they also sold straw fuses for use down the pit. The miners from Balaclava, Redan and Inkerman were great rivals, mostly in religion, and there are accounts that they fought pitched battles at Paisley Racecourse, which bordered on riots, with each other. Newspaper articles of the time report that 'heads were cracked and blood flowed freely.' In the 1970s the site was used for St Andrews Primary School, which was later renamed Our Lady Of Peace.

All that remains of Darluith is this part of a brick wall on the roadside to Houston. The name Darluith means 'Dark Meadow'. This was also a small mining community consisting of a couple of rows of houses. As well as the mines there was also a limekiln for burning lime. The wall remains as a reminder of a way of life that has passed into fading memories.

Three
Local Mansions

Burnbrae House, home to the Spiers family.

Blackston House had several spellings – Blaxton, Blackstone, or Blackstoune. Built by Abbot George Shaw in the late fifteenth century on the north bank of the River Black Cart about a mile downstream from Linwood, it was used by Paisley Abbey as a grange where the locals paid their tithes by cash, poultry, labour and share of their crops. The house was then acquired by the Earl of Abercorn by a charter dated 29 July 1587. The Earl, in turn, sold it to Sir Patrick Maxwell of Newark in 1653. Upon the death of Sir Patrick, his son John inherited the estate. John Maxwell had only one daughter, Catherine, to whom the estate was passed to upon his death. Catherine married Alexander Napier, whose father, John Napier, was the renowned mathematician who invented logarithms. Alexander demolished the old grange and built a new mansion in its place. Alexander followed a military career and rose to be a captain in the Scots Guards. During the 1745 rebellion he made himself conspicuous by being in charge of the local militia opposed to Bonnie Prince Charlie. When the Prince's troops were in Glasgow they paid Blackston House a visit and in reprisal plundered the house. Alexander died in 1751 and was succeeded by his son who was also named Alexander. He too followed the military calling and became a captain in the Foot Guards. In 1768 he sold his commission and returned to Blackston. After his death, his son Alexander III fell heir to the estate and like his father and grandfather, took up soldiering and became a lieutenant colonel in the 92nd Highlanders, unfortunately falling at the battle of Corunna in 1809. Alexander III was succeeded by his brother William, who went into banking and lost his fortune. In 1843 the estate was sold to Thomas Spier of Burnbrae. The house was demolished by the Pinkerton family between the wars and now only a small part of the servants' wing remains.

Burnbrae House was built in the tudor-gothic style, *c.* 1830, possibly by renowned architect David Hamilton. The house stood on the south bank of the River Black Cart and was owned by the Spiers family who had made their fortune in tobacco and were known as 'Tobacco Lords'. The man standing on the left is head gardener John Gilmartin, the others are the butler, maids and at the right-hand side stands a carriage with two ladies being escorted into it. One of women is Lady Anne Spiers, who was responsible for reviving the art of Houston Embroidery, at that time a cottage industry. On her death she was interred in the family vault below Linwood parish church. She is said to have placed a curse on the village, stating that a great disaster would befall the village if ever she or the church were ever disturbed. The grounds were used for fetes, gatherings and surrees (soirees). The house was demolished around 1940.

The lodge at Burnbrae stood at the roadside just opposite the manse on the left-hand side, coming into the village, and at one time was the abode of the head gardener, Mr Gilmartin, who also had a street named after him. The lodge, like the house, has been demolished.

Clippens House. The name dates back over 1,000 years. The lands of Clippens had been in the hands of the Cochran family since the middle of the fifteenth century and the house has a dark and sinister past. Legend has it that Steven Cochran was working on the roof of his house when he heard a voice calling his name from the trees. The voice was 'auld mahoun', the Devil, in the form of a magpie, asking Steven to release him from this guise and in return he could have anything he wanted. Steven agreed, removed his hat, and after making a hole in the crown, placed it over the chimney. He then asked the Devil to fill his hat with gold. As the hat filled with the gold, he fell through the hole, down the chimney and began filling up the room with gold. While the Devil was engaged in this, Steven jumped round and clipped a piece out of his sooty tail – this is how the Devil came by his forked tail and how Clippens was named. Steven then became known as 'cheat the deil.' Fiction? Maybe! The fact is that in 1650 Steven Cochran was taken to the session at Kilbarchan and charged with 'practising witchcraft and necromancie'. He was incarcerated in Paisley Abbey in a room now known as 'Stiens-Stevens-Chamber'. His uncle, the Earl of Dundonald, was a powerful man who used his considerable influence on the authorities to have his nephew freed, who, in turn, paid his uncle with a 'skinful' of gold. Was this the Devil's gold? The present house was built in 1817 by Dr Peter Cochran and has had several owners down the years, including the Sheriff Substitute for Scotland, mill owners, factory owners and in the 1960s was used by the Civil Defence as a command centre. It has recently been converted into flats. The house is haunted by a white lady who is seen on a regular basis in the surrounding area.

Clippens House in 1959, when its owners were the Howden family, who owned a large engineering factory in Glasgow. By this time a new wing had been added to the east side of the house. The Howdens were generous benefactors to good causes in the community with Mrs Howden donating a new organ to the church.

The inscribed lintel from the older Clippens House reads:

'This house is built by John Cochran of Clippings Hall – August the 22nd 1744'.

The ruins of this building were demolished in the 1990s to make way for a housing development. The remains of the inscribed lintel can be seen built into the low wall on the left of the entrance into the estate.

Caigends House on the south bank of the River Gryffe. The name means the rock of the meadow. This has been the seat of the Cunningham family since the land was granted to William Cunningham by his father Alexander, the first Earl of Glencairn, in 1479. The house in the picture was described by Crawfurd in 1710 as 'imposing, adorned with pleasant orchards and gardens'. The house looked more like a castle because of the need for constant defence from enemies, of which the Cunninghams had no shortage.

Built in 1857 to replace the old Craigends House, the new one was palatial by comparison. The architect was David Bryce, RSA, and the house was thought by many to be his best Scots baronial mansion and his finest country house. The Cunninghams had a long and bloody feud with the Montgomerie family, which lasted over 150 years. In 1533, the second laird, William, and his manservant, Robert Allansoun, were slain as they returned home up the tree-lined drive to the house. Five people were later convicted and beheaded for their part in the murders. The third laird, Gabriel, was killed at the battle of Pinkie on 10 September 1547. In later years other lairds were representatives in the Scottish Parliament as well as being County Justices and distinguished soldiers. In addition to owning several estates in Renfrewshire, Alexander, the eleventh baron, owned properties in the West Indies. Alexander laid out new gardens and orchards along with the lime tree avenue and also grew tobacco in five acres of his policies growing tobacco. The Cunningham line came to an end with John Charles, the thirteenth generation since 1477. In the late 1960s the house fell into a state of dereliction and was demolished in 1975 to make way for a private housing development.

The main entrance to Craigends was the last part to be demolished. The stone lion on the top was saved and is now standing proudly at the front of what was the old school in Houston.

Amid the rubble of Craigends House is one of the many biblical inscriptions that adorned the building.

Linwood House was situated in Napier Street and built by the Watsons, who owned the paper mill. They moved out to live in Johnstone Castle and the manager of the mill moved in. In the early 1970s it was last owned by Mr Brian Hick, a local man who had a coach hire business. He sold it and a short time later it was demolished. The site is now a small private housing estate.

This house, although not quite a mansion, is of local interest. Its name is West Fulwood House and it lies just on the north bank of the Gryffe and south of the Georgetown Road. It was used in 1996 to film the television series *Dr Findlay's Casebook*, and the name Arden House can be seen on the gate pillar. In the garden there is a stone seat which has an lintel inscribed with the date 1711, which came from the original Fulwood House.

Walkinshaw House stood at the confluence of the Rivers Gryffe and Black Cart about half a mile downstream from Blackston House. For centuries this was seat of Walkinshaw of that Ilk, as they obtained the land from the monks of Paisley Abbey in 1235. The name Walkinshaw of that Ilk was linked to Prince Charles Edward Stewart through Clemintina Walkinshaw, whom the King of France created Countess of Alberstrof. Her daughter Charlotte was created Duchess of Albany by the Bonnie Prince. The estate remained in the Walkinshaw family until 1769, when it was acquired by the Millar family who held it for eighty years before it passed to the Cunninghams of Craigends. The house was designed by Adam and was unusual in its octagonal shape. The Cunninghams owned coal and ironstone pits in Blackston and Inkerman, and these mining operations brought about the downfall of the house. Cracks began to appear in its structure both inside and out until it became dangerous and had to be demolished.

Four
Churches

The Parish Church, c. 1900. Looking west down Napier Street.

Linwood parish church was built in 1860 as a chapel of ease. Prior to this the villagers had to travel to Kilbarchan parish church as Linwood came under that parish at that time. The foundation stone was laid on 18 June 1859 and a box containing coins and newspapers of the day were placed in a cavity. The builder was David Jeffery of Johnstone, while the first minister was the Revd James Wallace from Lochwinnoch. The population had steadily increased to 2,750 in 1871 and the local heritors and people of standing presented a petition to Kilbarchan session requesting that the church be granted a status of *Quoad Sacra*, which was finally granted on 19 January 1880. The small building on the right is the half-time school and the buildings on the left were built for railway workers. By the 1960s the population had rocketed to eight times its 1871 number and a new church was built in 1965 in Clippens. The old church lingered on until it was demolished in the late 1970s. Lady Ann Spiers, who lay in her family vault below, had placed a curse on the village by saying a great disaster would befall it if she or the church were ever to be disturbed. About five years later her prediction came true when the car factory closed with the loss of thousands of jobs.

The Revd Dr Robert Graham MA DD, 1847-1895. The Revd Graham was the minister in Kilbarchan at the time the chapel of ease was built and gave a speech at its opening. He also helped make the decision to grant it *Quoad Sacra* status in 1880.

The Revd James Douglas, 1867–1873, was a missionary and the second minister. He was born in Dundee and after a short stay of six years he moved to Kinning Park, Glasgow.

The Revd John Adamson Abernethy, 1880-1926. Born in Parkhead, Glasgow, the Revd Abernethy was ordained in September 1880 and was married in September 1886 to Margaret Arneil. They had two sons, Peter and William. John retired in 1926 after serving the people of Linwood for forty-six years and moved to Fairlie in Ayrshire, where he died in 1936. He is buried in the Abbey cemetery, Elderslie.

The Revd Alexander Reaper, MA, 1927-1935. Born in Aberchirder, Banffshire, he was inducted in 1927 and the first baby he baptised was named Alexandrina Reaper. Alexander moved to Kirriemuir, Angus in 1935, where he retired in 1958 and died in 1966. Behind him is the pavilion of the Linwood Bowling Club, with the old cotton mill buildings on the left.

The Right Revd Andrew Herron BD, LLB, was the sixth minister and was inducted in January 1936. In 1971 Revd Herron became the Moderator of the General Assembly of the Church of Scotland. He is now retired.

The interior of the old parish church, c. 1950.

The new church hall, opened in October 1951, is seen here from the north side.

The old manse at Linclive. Built to house the minister, it was actually just outside the village in the Abbey parish of Paisley. It is now a private residence.

The new manse on the left was built on the site of the old parish church. The new hall is on the right and is used by a local shopkeeper for storage.

The new parish church, built in Clippens Road, was dedicated in February 1965. The foundation stone was laid by Mr Robert Leitch who had been session clerk for thirty-three years. At the time of construction the church was widely criticised for its unchurchlike architecture and was described as a warehouse, or an extension of the car factory. Some of these opinions have mellowed over the years but, since the bell was removed from its tower, it looks even less churchlike.

The RC Chapel/School was established as a mission in 1865 in Napier Street, with an average of forty-five pupils. Mass was said every month. By 1881 the average attendance had reached ninety-seven and plans were made to extend the mission building. Later that year it had doubled in size.

In 1896 a small wooden church was constructed in Inkerman and dedicated to Saint Milburga (a Saxon princess from Shropshire) to whom Paisley Abbey had also been dedicated. As the Roman Catholic population had expanded, mainly due to the influx of Irish immigrants, the small wooden church was moved from Inkerman to Linclive where it was used until the building of the new chapel which then opened on 6 November 1932. The new church was dedicated to Saint Conval, while the old wooden church then became the church hall. When the second church opened in 1967, the church built in 1932 was converted to Saint Conval's Social Club.

The interior of Saint Conval's, c. 1950.

Built on the site of the former Greenfarm in Bridge of Weir Road, the second church of Saint Conval had its foundation stone laid by Bishop Black, on 12 September 1966. It was officially opened on 2 June 1967. A feature and local landmark of the church was its bell tower surmounted by a triple cross. In the 1970s, cracks began appearing in its structure and a slight lean was noticeable. The experts who examined it recommended demolition, but events were taken out of their hands when a violent storm arose during the night and the tower was sent crashing down across the main road. Thankfully, there was no real damage done to any persons or property. Was this action divine intervention?

The Presbytery stood opposite the manse at Linclive. On the right can be seen the old wooden church. When the new church opened in 1967, new accommodation was included for the priests.

Curate Revd Kieran Gallacher, 1956-1958. When Kieran arrived he did secretarial work for Bishop Black, which he left to do full-time in 1958.

Curate Revd Matt Dillon, 1958-1961. The Revd Dillon came from Saint Mary's in Greenock and left after three years to return to Portrush in Northern Ireland.

Curate Revd Sylvester McGrady, 1961-1962. A former chaplain in the Royal Navy and a curate in Port Glasgow. He left for Ireland in 1962.

Father Joseph Hamil, parish priest 1956-1963. Father Hamil came from Bishopton to Linwood. He died in October 1963 after suffering from a long illness.

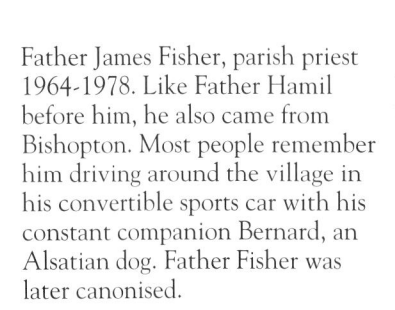

Father James Fisher, parish priest 1964-1978. Like Father Hamil before him, he also came from Bishopton. Most people remember him driving around the village in his convertible sports car with his constant companion Bernard, an Alsatian dog. Father Fisher was later canonised.

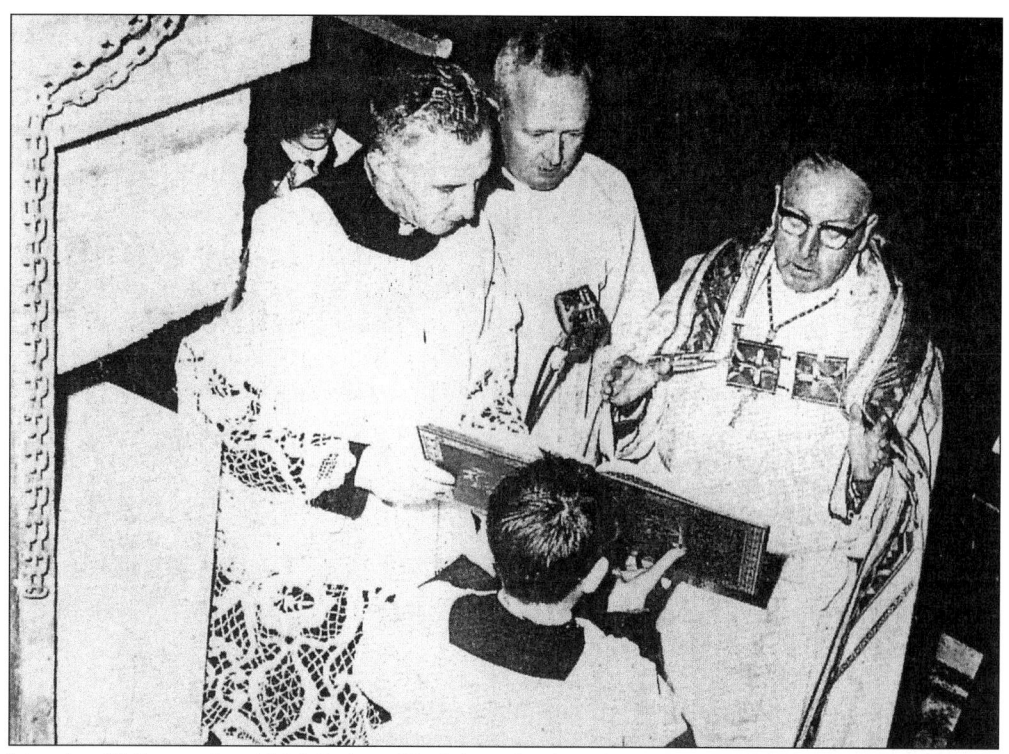

Monday 12 September 1966, Bishop Black lays the foundation stone of the new church.

A large crowd of parishioners watch the laying of the foundation stone. Note the raised umbrellas as the church did not have a roof at this time.

The Brethren Hall in Bridge Street. Before this gospel hall was built, the Brethren met in the band hall in Napier Street.

The Baptist church in Erskinefauld Road. It was built around 1974 near the site of the old chemical works which had been destroyed by fire a number of years earlier.

Five
Streets and Buildings

Bridge Street, seen from Duke Street, c. 1965. The Co-op building is on the right, adjoining Greenhill Terrace. The gentlemen is James McCrudden.

Armour Place in Bridge Street, decorated for the 1953 Coronation. The building was demolished in the 1960s.

Napier Street looking east and decorated for another coronation, this time in 1937. Behind the group on the left is Galbraith's shop, The Tavern, and beyond that is Agnes Stevenson's shop.

Looking across the intersection of Bridge Street to Napier Street, *c.* 1900.

Before the Old Cart Bridge was built in 1776, the only way across the River Black Cart was by stepping stones. After its construction, the way to trade was opened up and industry followed in the shape of two cotton mills, a print mill and engineering works. On Saturday 12 July 1859, the miners from The Redan in Linwood and rivals from Inkerman met in the Battle of Linwood Bridge when factions from both sides fought out a bloody fight. One man was killed and several were badly injured, with weapons varying from mining tools, swords and cudgels, to anything which came to hand. The bridge was renovated in 1911 and is still in use today.

The Old Cart Bridge, c. 1914. A popular gathering place for the villagers to have a 'wee blether'. On the right-hand side is the home farm for Burnbrae House.

Bridge Street, c. 1900. Over the bridge the first houses on the left are Holm Terrace, Burnbrae Terrace, the police station, Lee Place and Charlie Pattison's smiddy.

Napier Street, 1900, looking east with Dunlop Street on the right, just opposite 'the burnt end'. A crowd has gathered at the junction of Bridge Street, possibly for a parade of some sort.

Napier Street was always the centre of village life with small groups in conversation exchanging news or gossip.

New Houses, Linwood

In 1920 when this picture was taken, these houses in Bridge of Weir Road were new. The village was beginning to expand towards the Greenfarm. North and South Drives were on the left and right as we look at this photograph.

Burnbraë House Home Farm was taken over by the paper mill and converted into office accommodation, with sectional wooden annexes being added. In the mid-1970s the whole lot was demolished and the site is now used as a lorry park.

These cottages at the foot of Napier Street belonged to the owners of the cotton mill. The small window on the right was used as a docket and pay office. The cottages still survive but are now used as homes.

Looking north from high up in the paper mill in the 1940s. The school on the left was then Saint Conval's Primary and formerly the public school. Above the school is Dunlop Street and, on the right, the big house is Redlea, built by W. J. Hart Reid who owned the Reid Gear Company. It was, however, occupied by his manager James Lochhead. There is a long tradition in the village of naming streets after people who had a significant standing in the community. James Lochhead was granted this honour and we have Lochhead Avenue in his memory.

'Wee' Napier Street was used as a terminus for the bus service and is seen here in 1937 decked out for the coronation.

Andrew McAree and his collie Glen stand outside Lizzie Muggins' shop. In his younger years Andrew drove the sour milk cart. Muggins' shop moved further up Bridge Street when the old one was demolished around 1950.

The Telegraph Office in Napier Street with Agnes Thompson in the doorway. The notice in the window is advertising the letting of seats in the parish church.

The Telegraph Office moved to new premises round the corner in Bridge Street, seen here in the 1950s. A decade later it was to be converted to a fish & chip shop. The owner Domenic Di Ciacca opened another chip shop in the new shopping centre and the old one was demolished A shop unit with a house above it was built in its place. (see next photograph)

The building on the right is San Remo City, built on the site of the old post office. The houses on the left are in Park Place. When this photograph was taken in 1975 it was semi-derelict. Unlike most of the old houses they escaped demolition and have now been renovated. They stand as the last remaining buildings of old Bridge Street.

Looking down from Dunlop Street towards Bridge Street. The Co-op gala parade gathers outside the Co-op building before marching behind the Johnstone Silver Prize Band down to the public park where the festivities took place. On the right is the Masonic Hall. The chimney in the distance is from the chemical works. Greenhill Terrace is on the left.

Napier Street, c. 1976, looking east towards the now unused parish church above which some scaffolding can just be seen, indicating that the high flats were under construction. On the right is The 'new' Tavern public house. The old one was converted into a bookmakers.

Napier Street, 1976. The large building in the centre was the old Co-operative halls. The small building on the left had many uses in its time as a dentists, doctors, opticians and from 1987 it was used by the Linwood Heritage Society and a quoiting club. Both buildings are now gone.

The Schoolmaster's House at the bottom of Napier Street. Built in 1879 and home to Matthew Mycroft, affectionately known as 'daddy' to all his scholars. Mycroft began as the schoolmaster in the old school in 1907 and moved to the new school in 1911, retiring in 1928 after twenty-one years in office. The house has been extended and is now the home of Mr & Mrs John Reid.

Bridge Street, 1976. On the left is the entrance to the shopping centre and behind the lorry is the Ponderosa public house.

The junction of Bridge of Weir Road and Moss Road in the early 1960s. The white gable end on the right is the Black Bull, which preceded the Ponderosa.

To the left of this scene was the site of the Blackburn Engineering Works. During the Second World War the factory made parts for Sunderland flying boats. The factory was latterly owned by Rubery Owen, who manufactured metal-framed windows and caravan chassis. On the right can be seen the bell tower of St Conval's church with its triple cross, which collapsed during a storm.

Barrowmanous Pit had several spellings but was widely called Barrowmans. It was another ironstone mine and suffered a great fire in 1880. Barrowmans cottage stood near the pit and is seen above with some of its residents.

Andrew McAree and Glen in Hart Street, c. 1950. In the background is the Black Bull known locally as 'Burns' Pub'.

Bridge of Weir Road, c. 1954. A procession of schoolchildren are led by a piper on the occasion of the Queen's visit to Paisley. She passed through Linwood en route to a function and the streets were lined by children waving and cheering. Opposite the school can be seen a row of haystacks at the Greenfarm.

North Drive, c. 1950.

Clippens Villa. Built by the Clippens Shale Oil Company in the 1880s. It later became the farmhouse of Mr J. Stirling and is now owned by Renfrewshire Council.

Johnstone Infectious Disease Hospital was built in Bridge of Weir Road, Linwood, in 1887 for the convenience of the people of Johnstone, hence the name. It had sixteen beds which in time of epidemics could be increased to thirty. There was also a matron's house, mortuary and a coach house for the horse-drawn ambulance. The prevalent diseases at the time were diphtheria, erysipelas, scarlet fever, enteric fever (typhoid), phthisis (consumption), pneumonia, whooping cough and measles. A ward was equipped with an operating theatre for patients with puerperal fever. Better standards in housing along with improved sanitation and powerful new drugs like sulphonamides, streptomycine and the vaccination of BCG, all meant that these diseases began to vanish. The hospital now caters for long-term chronically sick and elderly people.

Moss Cottage. Situated in Moss Wood and owned by the Elderslie Estates. It was at one time the home of the gamekeeper.

Fulwood Bridge crosses the Gryffe about half a mile beyond Moss Cottage. Built in 1861 it features a triple span design.

The weir on the Black Cart upstream from the Mill o' Cart. On the right is the start of the mill lade on its way to the paper mill. The houses in the background are in Kintyre Avenue, in front of which the new Howood bypass now runs.

Downstream from the above weir is the 'Shoogly Brig', so called because the original footbridge was made of wood with cross slats (a few of which were always missing, making it sway and wobble). The bridge was upgraded to steel and concrete in the 1960s but the winter floods can still make it impassable to pedestrians.

Mill o' Cart Bridge. This stone single span-bridge crosses the mill lade at Mill o' Cart Farm. The farm was demolished in the 1960s and the bridge suffered the same fate twenty years later to make way for the new Howood bypass.

Blackston Bridge, which spans the Black Cart, was erected in 1762 by Alexander Napier who lived in Blackston House.

Aerial view taken in 1954. From right to left: Holm Terrace, Burnbrae Terrace, the police station, Lee Place, then Allardyces' garage. To the right can be seen the Tomato Houses, which were started by a firm from Lanarkshire and covered seven acres. Behind the goalposts on the right is a shale bing from the Linclive Pit.

In the centre is the mill lade as it enters the paper mill, the tail-race can just be seen exiting on the right into the Black Cart. On the bottom left is the parish church.

From a high vantage point in the paper mill we look east. The lade is seen passing under Bridge Street as it comes into the mill. On its left is Allardyces' garage, formerly the blacksmiths, while on the right of the lade is a building called the 'three storey lawn'.

Candren Road seen from the mill, looking south. The two bungalows were built for the managers in the paper mill. Lang's Farm is just above that with a row of haystacks across the middle of the picture. Beyond them is the Army Camp, then Pressed Steel's factory.

Napier Street looking down from the mill, c. 1950. The large house on the right with the dormer windows is the Co-op building, the small light-coloured house is Renfrew's dairy, on the corner of Dunlop Street. Agnes Stevenson's newsagents is after that, then The Tavern and Galbraith's grocer shop.

Napier Square was built in 1880, and seventy years later it was demolished. One of the demolition workers can be seen standing on the first floor. The paper mill built an extension on the site.

Rab Brydson stands in front of the old half-time school in 'wee' Napier, prior to it being pulled down.

Bridge Street as seen from the window of a house in Holm Terrace, c. 1950. A Graham's bus is seen bound for the Hawkhead terminus in Paisley. Graham's bus service began in 1925 and was the only bus operator until deregulation in the 1980s. The firm ceased operations altogether in 1991.

Rab Brydson at the bus stop outside the Bucks Head Inn, while in the background someone looks into Lizzie Muggins' now semi-derelict shop.

The bus arrives at the Bucks Head Inn. From left to right: Rab Brydson, Mr Lauder the village lamplighter, or 'leerie', who went round the village lighting the gas streetlamps, then Louis Brown and Mr Horne.

The Old Fever Hospital later became the Combination Hospital and was named the Tin Hospital by the locals because of its construction from corrugated tin. It was situated in Muirhead and was equipped to allow the staff to remain on site as long as the outbreak lasted. Whenever a patient died, the body was placed on a trolley and wheeled to the end of the road, where it was left to await collection by the undertaker in his horse-drawn hearse, such was the fear of contamination. In the Second World War it was used to treat soldiers who contracted infectious diseases while in the area. In the 1950s it housed the homeless and transient workers before it fell into a state of disrepair and was renovated in the 1970s, as seen in the above photograph. After all this it was set on fire by vandals and destroyed.

Erskinefauld Road at the junction of Greenfarm Road as seen from the top of the Fullwood Bing. On the left is Jessie Mackie's shop which began life on the site in a wooden hut. The houses in the front are in Kinnaird Drive. During the Second World War the locals watched the Clydebank Blitz when the Luftwaffe bombed the town. The bing was removed in the late 1960s and Erskinefauld Road began to subside into the old mineworkings around 1973.

Clippens Road in 1976. The small house on the right is the lodge to Clippens Estate, which at that time was a Civil Defence Command Centre to be used in the event of a nuclear disaster. Clippens House was under the command of Wing Commander Johnstone, who lived in the Coach House. Johnstone kept a log of all the strange happenings and events in Clippens House including poltergeist activity. He is said to have met the 'White Lady' personally on at least one occasion and was stricken with fear. On the right is the Bull Park where the farmer's prize bull was kept. It is now a bus terminus with a public convenience built in the park. The lodge at Clippens was demolished in the 1990s to make way for a private housing development.

Linwood Town Centre as visioned by the planners and architects in the 1960s. It was to include a regional shopping centre, library, community hall, clinic and parking for hundreds of cars. Part of Hart Street was demolished to accommodate this plan. The circular building on the left was meant to be a hotel with a revolving restaurant. This fell through literally, as the ground was unsafe due to the old mineworkings and subsided into a hole. The multi-storey flats were reduced – instead of three, only two were built on the site of the old Linwood Brickworks and Barrowmans Pit. The space for parking cars was also reduced, and even today the shopping centre was never the success they had planned, with units never occupied in thirty years.

Six
Social and Leisure

A group of local 'worthies' enjoy a seat at Dent's Corner, September 1968. They are from left to right: J. Heron, Rob Ewing, Bennet McGroarty, Albert Pearson, Mick Brown, Shawn Black, Willie Scarff, Colin Richmond.

Linwood parish church choir, c. 1900. After a visit to the birthplace of poet Robert Burns, the choir are seen here at the 'Auld Brig' at Alloway. They are from left to right, back row: Maxwell Stevenson, Maggie Galbraith, Rowan Prentice, -?-, Lizzie Taggart, John Gilmartin, Jeannie Wilson, Annie Ross. Middle, sitting: Annie Gilmartin, Robert Cochrane (organist), Anne Prentice, John Prentice, Maggie Prentice, Tommy Prentice, Liza Prentice. Front: -?-, Mary Prentice, Nellie Clark.

Linwood parish church outing to the Pencil at Largs, Ayrshire. From left to right, back row: Mary McCurday, John Gilmartin, ? Wilson, May Donaldson, Lizzie Galbraith, -?-, Matthew Mycroft, -?-, Jenny Allison, Johnny Pattison, Jessie Galbraith, Lizzie Stevenson. Middle: John McCurday, Annie Murray, Jeannie Prentice, Martha Brydson, Revd J. Abernethy, Mrs J. Abernethy, Hannah Wilson, May Abernethy. Front: Tom Prentice, -?-, -?-, Famy Dickson, Martha McCurday, Isa Wright, Charlie Pattison Jnr, Jessie Murray, -?-, Annie Rowan.

Napier Street, 1897. The celebration of Queen Victoria's Diamond Jubilee. This group of mostly boys wear commemorative medals to mark the occasion. On the left, two members of the Linwood Flute Band can be seen in their uniforms. The man on the left holding his cap by his side is Rowan Prentice. The banner reads Linwood Thistle Lodge No. 191 BOA Free Gardeners' Society. The group was photographed in the grounds of Linwood House. The mill chimney and bell tower are just visible.

The same occasion but this is mostly girls and younger children standing on the lawn of Linwood House. With the exception of one or two, the children are all wearing hats.

Napier Square 1901. From left to right: Pauline Smith, Mrs Smith – Paulines mother, Agnes McMeekin with Lizzie Smith in front of her, Dave Smith, Agnes Hannah McCurday, Margaret McMeekin Snr (sitting), Margaret McMeekin Jnr (child), small boy Robert McMeekin, Jane McMeekin his mother.

Linwood Public Park, 1935, Sunday School outing. The man standing on the left is James Lochhead, manager of the Reid Gear Company. The man on the right is William Wilson the local joiner and undertaker.

The Paper Mill 'jant' or jaunt, c. 1950. This was an annual trip that went to most of the Scottish resorts. The first two people on the left are Loudovic Blackwood and Mary Muldoon. The first two on the right are 'Granny' Stevenson (the local midwife) and Peter Gavin.

A piper greets the arrival of the Mill jaunt. From left to right are: Christie Welsh, -?-, bus driver, Paddy Muggins, Mary Muldoon, Loudovic Blackwood, -?-, -?-, -?-, -?-.

Mr & Mrs Charles McCurday celebrate their golden wedding anniversary, c. 1880. It was a time when a golden wedding celebration was a rare occasion. From left to right, back row: Jean McCurday, John McCurday, Isobel McCurday, Willie McCurday, Mary McCurday. Middle: George McCurday, Charles McCurday, Jean McCurday, Ninian McCurday. Sitting: Penman McCurday, Agnes McCurday.

The Paper Mill Gardens. Jacob Wilson, on the right, tended these gardens next to what was the home farm for Burnbrae House. Jacob came from Strone in Argyll, his brother Tammy Wilson who was a pattern maker in the Reid Gear built the two houses at the corner of Bridge Street and Bridge of Weir Road. They were named Rosebank and Marne. The other man is Hugh (the lark) Larkin. The paper mill is behind them.

Napier Street, 1935, during the celebration of the silver jubilee of King George and Queen Mary. From left to right, back row: Mrs Cummings, Jane McMillan & son, Mrs Slavin, Mrs McQuade, Mrs Caldwell, Charlie Caldwell, Jimmy Caldwell, Mary Gray, Madge Haney, Mrs D. Hunter, Mr McGroarty, Helen Larkin. Front: Maggie Boyle & son William, Mrs Major, Lizzie McElhone, Bridget Conner. Sitting: Mick McQuade.

Linwood Public School, July 1953. A group of senior citizens enjoy a coronation tea. From left to right, front row: Mr Houston, Mr Morgan, -?-, -?-, -?-, Mr Stewart, Mrs Edmiston. Second row: Mr Wilson (Leerie), -?-, -?-, -?-, -?-, -?-, Mrs P. Scarff. Third row: Mrs Lennon, Mrs McKinstry, -?-, Mrs McSporran, Mr McSporran, Mrs Hanlon, Mr Hanlon, -?-, -?-, Greta McGovern, -?-, -?-. Back row: Mrs Caldwell, -?-, -?-, -?-, -?-, Mary Burns, -?-, -?-, Lizzie Muggins,

95

Paddy Muggins.

Retiral ceremony in the mill. From left to right, back row: Mrs Francis McAleer, Mrs Chris Wilson, Mr Knut Appold (Mill Manager), Willie McCallum, Mrs John Ingils, Mrs Dickson. Front: Mr Francis McAleer, Mr Chris Welsh, Agnes Rodger, Mr John Inglis, Mr Dickson.

A group of workers in the Tomato Houses in the 1950s enjoy a leisure break. From left to right, back row: -?-, Margaret Muggins, Aggie Duffy, Madge Muggins. Front: Margaret Craigie, Grace Murdoch, Jane McMillan, Rosie Tiffin, Mrs McQuade.

Bobby Prentice, 'Flesher', poses for the camera during a break. Bobby killed all his own beasts at the back of his premises. Every one in the village remembers his excellent sausages as well as his rather grumpy disposition! His daughter became a teacher in the local public school.

Jim Sweeney's football team. Mr Sweeney was the owner of the Black Bull Inn in Bridge Street. From left to right, back row: James Brydson, Willie Scarff. Third row: Davie Phillips, Tommy Rourke, -?-, Baden Powell Hamilton, Robert Tennant, Charlie Flynn (Trainer). Second row: Hugh Morgan, Jack Lochhead, Robert Reid, Peter Flynn, James O'Rourke, John McArthur, Charlie McCormack. Front row: Robert Caldwell, John Sweeney, William Heatherton.

Linwood Bowling Club. The club had its beginnings in Napier Street around 1893 and moved to its present site in 1901. This photograph shows the opening day in 1901. From left to right, back row: John McCurday, John Reid (son of W.J. Hart Reid), Johnny Flynn, Will Steel, Jimmy Ritchie, Bob Rodgers, Mr Smith, Hosea Clark, Joe Blair, Oliver Jack. Third row: -?-, John Gilmartin, Alex Smith, Alex Wright, Jack Lochhead, Willie Houston, John Donaldson, Revd J.A. Abernethy, Matthew Mycroft (Schoolmaster), P.C. David Donaldson, W.J. Hart Reid, Jackie Horsburgh (Paper Mill Manager), Will Aitken, Oliver Cochrane (owner of the foundry in Duke Street), Jimmy Lochhead (Reid Gear Manager), Peter Abernethy (Minister's son), Robert Leitch, George Caldwell, Mr Ritchie, -?-, -?-, Will Leitch, Mr McSporran, Alan Aitken. Second row: Jimmy Lauder, Jock McMenemy, Johnny Morisson, Jock Malcolm, Mrs J. Lochhead, Mrs J. Ritchie, Mrs O. Cochrane, Mrs Reid, Mrs M. Mycroft, Mrs Smith, Mrs Campbell, Mrs H. Clark, -?-. Front: Helen Barker, Jenny Allen, -?-, -?-, Annie Malcolm, Lizzie Smith, Milly Mycroft, -?-, Ellen Aitken, Maggie Houston, Isa Wright, Isa Storrie, Mrs A. McMeekin, Mrs Jack, Mrs Aitken, Mrs P. Watson, Alice Watson, Kate Bannen.

W.J. Hart Reid, on the right, watches as the skip crouches to guide in the next bowl during a lively game. The man standing with the pipe is John Gilmartin.

Linwood Bowling Green, *c*. 1940. The paper mill buildings in the background clearly shows the bell tower on the roof. The parish church never had a bell so every Sunday the mill bell was sounded to summon the villagers to church. The whole building was destroyed by a huge fire in the 1960s in which a fireman lost his life. The trees on the right hide Linwood House.

Linwood Saint Conval's Football Club, 1930-31. From left to right, back row: P. McGovern, James McElhone, John McCann, Harry McKinstrey, Pat McGivern Snr, Pat McGivern Jnr, Hugh Lennon Snr. Middle: Johnny O'Donnell (Trainer), Joe Rennie, J. McGuire, Sam Stevenson, Jimmy Wardhaugh, Frank McCafferty, Malcolm McDonald, Jimmy Carroll, Hugh McKendrick. Front: Rab Ward, Johnny Campbell, Eddie Monagle, George Caldwell, Willie Watson, John McFadzean, Arthur O'Neil.

Reid Gear Spurs Football Club, 1936. The team are pictured here in their new strips before a match against Lobnitz of Renfrew. Their manager was Jimmy McSporran. From left to right, back row: D. Millar, R. Leitch, ? Clark, R. Gray, A. Laird, A. McFarlane. Front: -?-, W. Leitch, D. Lang, R. Thompson, R. Williamson.

Linwood Redan Quoiting Club, 1992. Quoits had been a popular game in the village since the middle of the nineteenth century, but went into decline after the Second World War. A club was revived in 1988 with a pitch in Napier Street. This occasion was when the local club met the champions Birkenshaw from Larkhall in the first round of the Scottish Cup at home, eventually losing out to the ten times champions from Lanarkshire. From left to right, back row: Hugh Cunningham, Jock Sim, George Smith, Kenny Hay, William Falconer, Boyd Falconer, Davie Reid. Front: Davie Wreathman, William Winters, Robert Black, Matt Connelly, Alec Doey.

Quoits. 1990 Scottish Cup Final. The match was played at Linwood, between Glenburn Miners Welfare from Prestwick and Birkenshaw from Larkhall, who won a close match and celebrated winning the magnificent trophy for the eighth time. From left to right, back row: Charlie McCormick, Davie Millar, William Reid, Jock Sim, William Winters, Jim Hendren, Alex McEwan, Alex Millar. Front row: Jim Winters, William Falconer, Boyd Falconer, Kenny Hay, Hugh Cunningham, Davie Falconer, George Smith.

Linwood parish church fete, 1963. The adults are from left to right: John Clark (Elder), Revd Colin Morton, Robert Leitch (Session Clerk), Mrs C. Morton.

Linwood Public School football team, c. 1908. The man on the left in the uniform is Mr McLaren, the janitor, while schoolmaster Matthew ('daddy') Mycroft stands in typical pose with arms akimbo.

Seven
Institutions

School Dinner Ladies in Mossedge Primary, 1967. From left to right: Mary Inglis, -?-, Margaret Devlin, -?-, Pat McCauley, Agnes Chitticks, -?-.

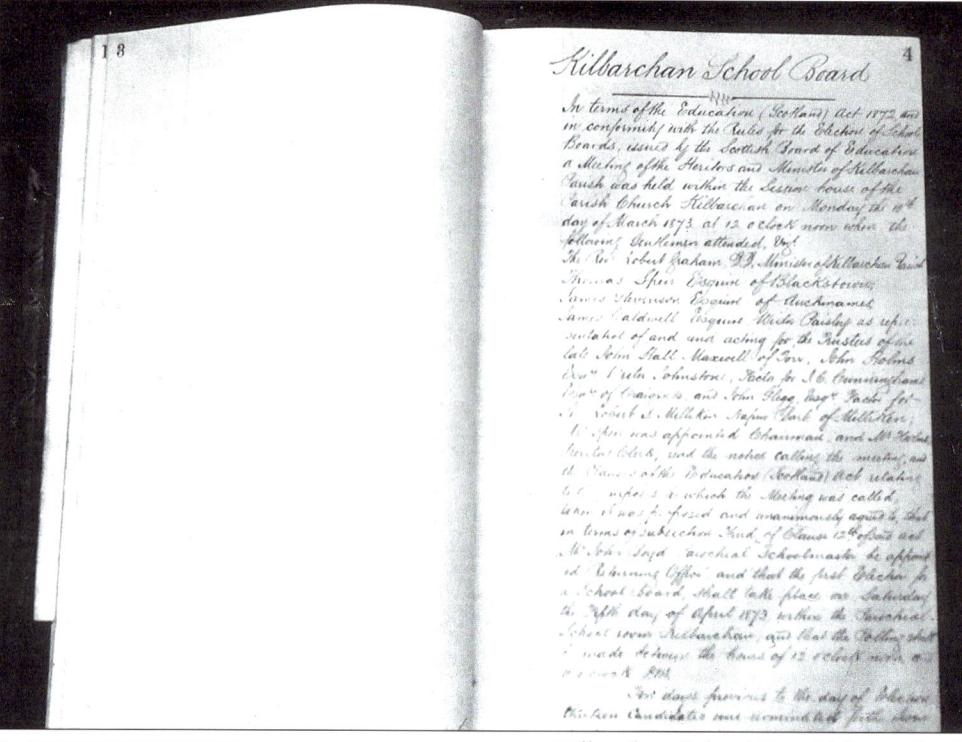

Kilbarchan School Board Minute Book, 10 March 1873. At this meeting the decision to build a new school was taken and the Board decided on Napier Street as the site. The school was opened on 12 June 1874 under Government inspection and the headmaster was Mr James Mitchell. There were 121 scholars made up of seventy-seven boys and forty-four girls on the register. This was increased when the school in Balaclava closed down and the pupils were transferred to Napier Street.

Page 13

List of Songs for Inspection
Thursday 15th March

Step to gether
The Royal Road
The lang awa' Ship
Blue Bells of Scotland
They're coming home to-day
Come soft and lovely evening
Waes me for Prince Charlie
Cold the blast may blow
Thou bonnie wood o' Craigielea
The boatie Rows
The harvest time
The silvery morn

15th March 1877

Annual Inspection present: 127

David Noo
L M J

The school was visited by the Government inspectors on a regular basis. This copy of the log book shows the songs the children were taught.

By the turn of the century the school was decaying badly and it was decided to build another one rather than spend a lot of money refurbishing the present school. The Roman Catholic Education Authorities offered the Board £650 for the school, this was accepted and it was duly renamed Saint Conval's Primary School. The new public school opened on Saturday 2 September 1911 on a site opposite the Green Farm in Bridge of Weir Road. The opening ceremony was performed by local heritor, Mr A. Hagart Spiers. He was presented with an inscribed golden key to mark the occasion. The first headmaster was Matthew Mycroft. The new school consisted of six classrooms, each entered from a large central hall, together with splendidly equipped rooms for cookery, laundry and woodwork. For the teaching of housewifery a sitting room, kitchen and bedroom were provided. There was also a female teachers' room along with a headmasters' room and a large cloakroom for boys and girls. These together with large playgrounds and outbuildings completed a school, which for its size could bear comparison with the most modern city school. On a downside, the parents often complained about the distance their children had to walk to reach the new school.

Linwood Public School, 1926. A small group of girls play 'Ring o' Roses' in the playground whilst a small barefoot boy looks on. The school later became known as the 'wee red school' due to the nature of its construction from red sandstone.

A class poses outside along with the headmaster Matthew Mycroft, c. 1920.

A class of girls dressed for their cookery and laundry lessons, c. 1920.

Miss Morrison's class, December 1912. Back row, second from the right is Bertie Boyle. Second row, fourth from left: Loudovic Blackwood. Third row, second from left: John Collinson. Front row, second from left: James Bell.

Teacher Liza Prentice with her class, c. 1933. The lad in the middle row, third from right is Robert Prentice.

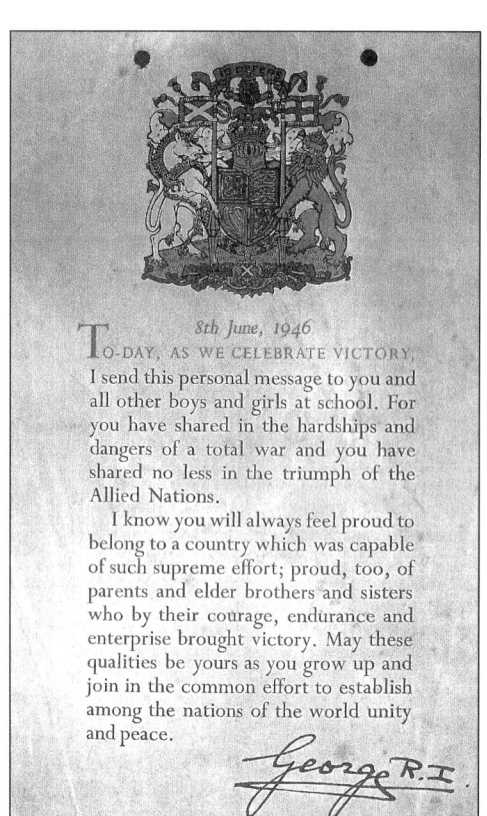

This personal message from King George VI was given to each boy and girl in every school in the land. On the rear it listed important war dates beginning with Hitler's invasion of Poland on 1 September 1939 to the British Forces re-entering Singapore on 5 September 1945. It also had a space to record your own family's war record.

> 8th June, 1946
>
> TO-DAY, AS WE CELEBRATE VICTORY, I send this personal message to you and all other boys and girls at school. For you have shared in the hardships and dangers of a total war and you have shared no less in the triumph of the Allied Nations.
>
> I know you will always feel proud to belong to a country which was capable of such supreme effort; proud, too, of parents and elder brothers and sisters who by their courage, endurance and enterprise brought victory. May these qualities be yours as you grow up and join in the common effort to establish among the nations of the world unity and peace.
>
> George R.I.

St Conval's school outing to Langbank, *c.* 1930. From left to right, back row: -?-, -?-, James Barr, John McGourlick, Annie Muggins, -?-, Father Dennehey, -?-, Sadie Welsh, -?-, Ellen McBride, -?-, Mary McKinstry, Mary McElhone, Miss Nora Weeple (Schoolmistress), Tommy McKinstry, -?-, Tommy Gray , -?-, -?-, Peggy Winters, -?-, Agnes Crampsey, -?-, Mary Boyle, -?-. Front: Mick Muggins, Frank McAleer, John McGowan, Andrew McAree, -?-, Terry McGowan.

St Conval's school outing to Langbank, 1931. From left to right, back row: Kate Corrigan, Alice Larkin, -?-, Mary Graham, Jeannie Connor, Rosanne McQuade, Mary Docherty, -?-, -?-, Rose Lyons, Nan McKinstry, -?-, -?-, -?-. Middle: Neil Carroll, Corneilius McColgan, Tom Edger, Jack Horan, -?-, John Slavin, Father Dennehey, Martha Morgan, Willie Gebbie, -?-, -?-, -?-, -?-, Jessie Gebbie, Miss Kelly. Front: Willie Cassidy, -?-, Charlie Brodley, Joe McBride, Frank Cassidy, -?-, -?-, -?-, John McCrudden, -?-, -?-, Sarah Donnelly. Lying down: Dan Carroll, -?-.

St Conval's church, c. 1930. Pictured outside the presbytery after making their first communion. From left to right, back row: Jim Horan, -?-, Margaret McAleer, Daniel Rennie, Isa McMillan, Mary Rafferty, Mick McQuade, Mary Broadley, Anna McKinstry, Danny Carroll, John Callaghan. Middle: Robert Corrigan, Margaret Conner, Winnie Graham, Jack Byrnes, Bridget McMahon, Agnes Kelly, Moses McGowan, Emile O'Neil, Margaret Donnelly, Chris Welsh, Bridget McGuinness, Mary McGuiness, Tommy Gray. Front: Isa McGlynn, Margaret McCann, Willie Taggart, Margaret Larkin, Annie McPherson, David Torrance, Marge McBride, Pat McGivern, Mary McCrudden, Lizzie McCrudden, John McCrudden, Jimmy Gray.

St Conval's school nativity play, 1954. From left to right, back row: Anna Marzejon, Patsy Lowe, Mary McFarlane, Carol Holman, -?-, Winnifred Lunn, Teresa Graham. Middle: -?-, -?-, Marie McMillan, Thomas McGowan, James McGourlick, Billy Slaven, Anne McMahon, Margaret Gillespie, Eileen Wright, Anna Muldoon, -?-, Rodger McCormick, Yvonne McGowan, Allan Hick, Florence McCormick, Jeanette Cunningham. Front: Eileen Linney, Marie Flood, Eddie McGowan, -?-, -?-, Brenda Lucas, Arthur Docherty, Arthur Graham, Harry Muggins, Patrick Paton, John McMenemy, -?-.

1st Clippens and 27th Renfrewshire Scout Troop, 13 August 1914. The boys proudly display their new bicycles in the grounds of Clippens House, whose owner had generously presented them to the troop. The Scoutmaster was Robert Collinson.

Linwood Home Guard in the grounds of Oakdene, Bridge of Weir Road, *c*. 1943. From left to right, back row: T. McGowan, J. Ritchie, G. Johnston, A. Barr, J. Deighan, T. McCormack, J. Slavin, R. Perrie, J. McCurday, T. Carroll, J. McVicar, J. McManus. Third row: W. Marshall, A. Collinson, W. Edmiston, J. Welsh, T. Cassidy, J. McManus, T. Caldwell, J. Anderson, W. Chalmers, W. Watson. Second row: P. Lennon, L. Cpl J. Thompson, Cpl W. Kerr, Cpl R. Stevenson, Lt A. Eaglesom, Lt F. Wilson MSM, Lt J. Pinkerton, Sergeant J. Dickson MM, Cpl R. Brown, L. Cpl C . McCurday. Front: J. Thompson, A. Eaglesom Jnr, T. McNeil, R. Picken, P. Mcgivern.

Private Hugh McIver VC, MM and Bar. Hugh's story begins in 1890 when he was born in Napier Street. He moved with his family when he was a young boy to Cambuslang near Glasgow. At the outbreak of the First World War he enlisted in the Second Battalion of the Royal Scots. In early actions he won the Military Medal twice and was later awarded the Victoria Cross for his heroic actions near Courcelle-Le-Compte in 1918. His citation reads; 'At great personal risk he saved many lives by stopping the fire of a British tank which was directed – in error – against our own troops at close range. Before performing that deed of salvation, then employed as a company runner, he had shown splendid courage in carrying messages in action, and he again proved his valour and resourcefulness when single-handed he pursued an enemy scout into a machine gun post, and after killing six of the garrison, he captured two machine guns and twenty prisoners.' He was sadly killed in action at Ypres charging a nest of machine guns. His VC was presented posthumously to his father at Buckingham Palace. Tragically, his father was killed in a pit accident only weeks later. His VC is now displayed at the Regimental Museum in Edinburgh Castle.

A Masonic outing, c. 1930. The Masonic Lodge Craigends No. 1042, began in May 1906 in Bridge Street. From left to right, back row: -?-, -?-, -?-, -?-, -?-, Revd Alexander Reaper, -?-, -?-, Robert Rodger. Middle: Matthew Ritchie, -?-, Hugh Smith, Alex Armit, -?-, Front: John Stark, John Malcolm, John Dickson, Robert Smith, -?-.

The Village Handbell. This bell was used up until 1872 by Jimmy Boyle who was the blind man in charge of the local village pump. He would ring the bell to announce that he had unlocked the pump and the villagers would turn out with their buckets to collect their daily supply. Sometimes, however, he would lock it up before they arrived and then shout 'the waals dry.' In 1872 a water supply was piped into the village from Paisley Water Works. The bell was also used by the local bellman (town crier) who went around the streets announcing all the latest news. The bell is now in the possession of the Galbraith Family.

Eight
The Car Plant

The Hillman Imp. First launched on 2 May 1963 by HRH Duke of Edinburgh KGKT at the official opening of the factory. The Imp had a 875cc, all-aluminium, overhead-camshaft engine that gave 45 miles to a gallon with a 0 - 60 time of 24.5 seconds and a top speed of 75 mph. There was synchromesh on all four gears, independent four-wheel suspension and 5,000 miles between services. In many ways it was more technically advanced than its competitor – the BMC mini. The Imp also gave the motoring world folding and split rear seats. However, despite its revolutionary developments, production ceased in 1976 – a victim of too much technology too fast.

Rootes Car Plant under construction in 1961-1962. The large group of factory buildings in the centre is the Pressed Steel Company Ltd. It was formally William Beardmore's Ltd and operated as a cover munitions works in 1941 in case of bomb damage to the Sheffield plants and gunworks. Beardmore's was a gigantic heavy engineering concern. After the Second World War the factory was taken over by the Pressed Steel Company who manufactured railway rolling stock and car body panels. In 1960 the Rootes Group in conjunction with the Pressed Steel announced a £22 million investment to produce a 'high quality people's car of quite unusual design.' The new factory when completed would cover 450 acres with 3,000,000 square feet of industrial floor space.

Railway rolling stock at the Pressed Steel Company, c. 1969. The company at its height made nine out of ten coal wagons in the UK, as well as one 16 ton mineral wagon every twelve-and-a-half minutes, in addition to hopper, ballast, sleeper and flat wagons. The famous blue trains were built between 1953-1957, together with refrigerated trailers, war department trailers, atlas crane bodies, rear fuselages and tail cones for the Hawker Hunter jet fighters and, in 1959, a small Austin van. The wagon in the picture was possibly the last one made before Rootes terminated all these contracts in 1969. Someone has chalked 'the end' on the buffers.

Welders at work on the chassis of a wagon. The large circular object is a trunnion jig which allowed the chassis to be turned upside down to enable easy access to awkward corners.

Patternmakers at work on the body of a Volvo P1800 sports car. The P1800 gained fame in the TV series *The Saint* when it was driven by Roger Moore. Other car bodies made there included a whole range of truck cabs for BMC and the Rover 3.5, as well as 2,000 Imp bodies a week.

The old Army Camp on the south east of Linwood Road is razed to the ground on 8 June 1961 in preparation for the new car plant, seen here from the Pressed Steel. The Linwood Road bisects the picture from left to right – work had not yet begun on the opposite side of the road.

The west gate entrance in 1964. The building on the left is the Personnel Department of Employment. The building with the Rootes sign is the main administration offices and showroom.

Looking towards Linwood Toll, c. 1967. A car transporter on the left heads for the factory, while the overhead transporter bridge spans the road between the east and west plants. The sign proclaims ROOTES (Scotland) Ltd, HOME OF THE HILLMAN IMP.

This car never went into production as it was a styling exercise around 1967.

A wheel arch is electronically welded by machine.

Gate line body build.

Gate line body build where the sides join the bottom floor pan.

Imp body shells on the overhead line.

A Hillman Avenger gets its first undercoat as it is lowered into an electro-phoretic paint dip. Production of the Avenger was transferred to Linwood in 1976.

A Sunbeam is lowered onto the engine and driveshaft.

A Hunter body shell is checked for alignment faults. Production of the Hunter was transferred to Linwood from Ryton in 1971.

A Chrysler Sunbeam comes off the assembly line. Production of the Sunbeam began in 1977.

Chrysler Sunbeam GLS.

Hillman Avenger GLS.

Hillman Avenger GL Estate.

Chrysler Sunbeam LS.

The plant was finally closed on 22 May 1981 after a long and weary fight to save it from closure. This was the last part to be demolished – an early victim of Thatcher's industrial strategy. The site has now been redeveloped with superstores, retail outlets, fast food chains, cinemas and a host of car sales premises – the 'pheonix has risen from the ashes'.

Nine
Inkerman

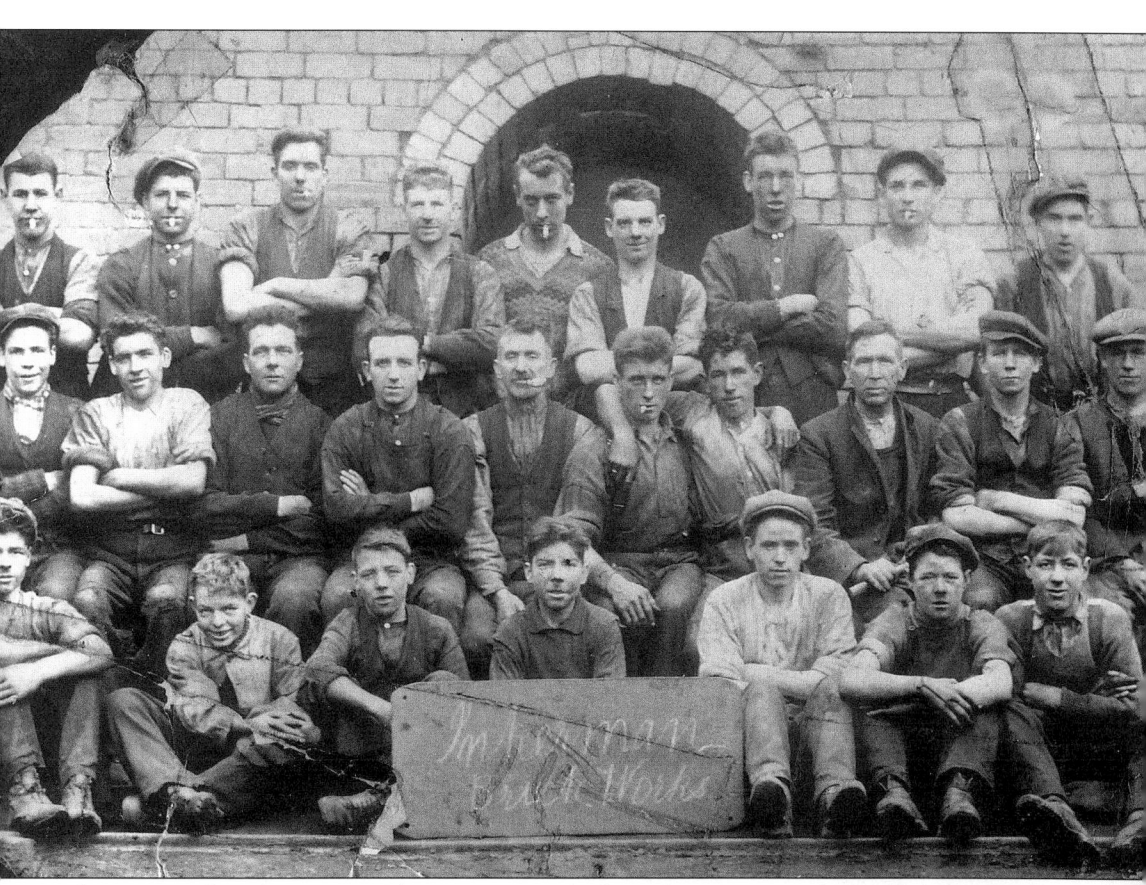

Inkerman Brickworks, c. 1930. The group consists of mostly young men, with a front row of all teenage lads.

The village of Inkerman stood about one mile east of Linwood. Built in 1854-1855, by Messrs Merry & Cunningham, who were local coal and ironmasters, the village was named after the Battle of Inkerman in the Crimean War. There were sixteen mines in the area with seven in Inkerman, which was rich in ironstone. The village consisted of five rows of houses, a company store, and later a school and schoolhouse were added along with reading rooms. There was no electricity, lighting was with paraffin lamps, heating was coal fires and the toilet was out the back. The picture is the store row with the company store being the higher part of the building – this had the luxury of running water. When the pits closed at the turn of the century, brickworks opened up at Blackston, Walkinshaw and Inkerman. In the 1930s, Merry & Cunningham went into liquidation and the village was put up for sale. The school closed in 1938 with the pupils being transferred to Linwood. When no one bought the village it was demolished and the population was split between Linwood and Elderslie, where they settled down. The school and its house remain as a testimony to a past life and a community now gone but not forgotten.

The rows each shared a well where the days supply was drawn. Here Jean McCrudden is rinsing her vegetables in a colander at the well, dressed in the typical pinnie of the time.

The Orr family, c. 1890. The Orrs stayed at No. 28 Second Row. James Orr with his wife Isabella Hardy Orr. Their daughter Georgina is on the left and their son George is on the right. Isabella wears a 'thibbet' apron while James wears his waterproof leggings worn down the pit in his work as an ironstone miner. Hanging on the wall of the house is his canary, which would be taken underground to act as an early warning signal of dangerous gasses.

A view of the rows, c. 1900. This group of women and children crowd in front of the camera to pose (most of the children are barefoot). Their menfolk would be at work down the pits.

A group of workers stand in front of a railway wagon, probably at the brickworks. The boy second from the right is James McCrudden.

Inkerman Rangers FC, winners of the Paisley and District League and Cup, 1908/09 and 1909/10. In their leisure time the miners liked their sports, mostly of the physical variety like quoits, with football being the big favourite. The small club produced many fine players with one of the most notable being Charlie Pringle who went on to play for local side St Mirren. In 1920 he moved to Manchester City where he played with the great Billy Meredith, starring with him in the 1926 FA Cup Final against Bolton. He then went on sign for Bradford City and married Meredith's daughter Lily.